Rosicrucianism

A Guide to Understanding the Philosophy and Ancient Wisdom

Table of Contents

Introduction..5

Chapter 1: The Birth of Rosicrucianism ..8

The Origin of Rosicrucianism 8

The Significance of the Term "Rosicrucianism" 11

Cultural Movement 13

Spiritual Movement.................................... 16

Chapter 2: What Does It Mean to Be a Rosicrucian? 19

Rosicrucian Vows and Obligations 19

Obligations 21

Gnosticism.................................... 24

Hermeticism.................................... 25

Gnosticism vs. Hermeticism 27

Chapter 3: Rosicrucian Organizations and Manifestos.................................... 29

Three Early Rosicrucian Societies................. 29

Primary Beliefs of Rosicrucian Organizations.. 30

Rosicrucian Manifestos 33

The Chymical Wedding of Christian Rosenkreutz.................................... 37

Chapter 4: The Rosicrucian Sign............**39**

The Sign of the Rose Cross...........................39

The Rose 41

The Cross 42

The Rosy Cross 44

Chapter 5: Rosicrucianism Today **47**

The Evolution of Rosicrucianism.................. 47

How Rosicrucianism Is Perceived Today......49

How Rosicrucianism Is Molded Today.........50

How Rosicrucianism Is Traced from the Past ...51

What Are the Modern Rosicrucianism Beliefs? 53

Conclusion **56**

References **59**

Introduction

Have you ever heard of the Rosicrucian Order? This intriguing society has fascinated and captivated many for centuries, but what exactly does it mean to be a part of this group? What is the story of its creation, who are its members today, and what are their beliefs?

A mysterious movement that began in Germany during the early 17th century, the Rosicrucian Orders have been active for over 400 years. Their teachings have sparked the imaginations of men for generations, with their symbol representing secrets and mysteries to be unlocked. This guide will explore what Rosicrucianism is, what they believe in, who their historical leaders and founders are, where you can find them today, and what teachings or practices define this mysterious movement.

You'll learn that the Rosicrucian Order is one of the most secretive and elusive groups in human history. Founded on principles of secrecy and mystery, it has inspired awe, fear, and rumors of its members having magical powers. Its symbols are still hotly debated today. Proponents believe that its teachings hold profound wisdom for mankind, while detractors argue that the Rosicrucians are a group of delusional mystics.

This guide will explore Rosicrucianism, its history, and the major Rosicrucian Orders.

The first chapter of this guide will serve as an introduction to Rosicrucianism. It will discuss the historical and cultural context in which Rosicrucianism began and give a brief history of its major events and figures. The second chapter will define and describe what Rosicrucianism is, its core teachings, and ideas. It will explain Rosicrucian vows and responsibilities and how they are used to shape followers' beliefs. This chapter will cover the two main paths of this movement- Gnosticism and Hermeticism, and the beliefs they convey.

The third chapter will introduce some major Rosicrucian Orders and discuss their history, membership, and specific teachings. It will talk about the most significant organizations and how they influenced the movement. Chapter four is dedicated to the importance of The Rose Cross, which is the Rosicrucian Symbol, and its prevalence. It'll talk about the individual elements in the sign - the Cross and the Rose, and how both collectively merge to become this powerful sign.

Finally, the fifth chapter will discuss how Rosicrucianism is viewed and practiced today and what individuals can gain from its study. At the end of this guide, you will better understand the basic tenets and ideas behind Rosicrucianism. Does it still hold the same importance and heaviness? How are modern Rosicrucianism beliefs molded, and how are they traced from the past?? What are the modern practices and teachings? This guide will answer such questions and allow you to make your conclusions about this ancient movement.

This guide does not go into the deep, everlasting questions of life. It doesn't explain how to follow a path of self-actualization and self-awareness; it does not explain the science of spirituality. This guide aims to understand the history and teachings of why this movement is well known. If you want to know how it relates or doesn't relate to modern-day beliefs, if you want to know what applications it has, or if you are curious about meditation, or if you are interested in joining the Rosicrucians, read on.

Chapter 1: The Birth of Rosicrucianism

What if we could live in an enlightened society without crime, violence, war, poverty, and greed, or selfishness? What if we found a way to remove all the disadvantages that face us today?

Rosicrucianism refers to a spiritual and cultural movement founded on esoteric principles. It is a philosophy and way of life that was first established by a secret society called the "Fraternity of the Rose Cross" in late medieval Germany to reconcile the emerging scientific discoveries with the spiritual life of humanity. This chapter will explore the emergence of this cultural and spiritual movement.

The Origin of Rosicrucianism

There are several different stories of the origin of the Rosicrucian Order as an organization. The first is about a German philosopher and physician called Christian Rosenkreuz. He made a pilgrimage to the Middle East, where he studied with Sufi masters, and on his return to Europe, he was unable to find a European teacher with adequate knowledge. He subsequently moved to the West Indies, where he wrote a book on alchemy titled The Chymical Marriage, which foretold the coming of a "Universal Reformation" based on esoteric truths buried under centuries of dogma.

In 1614, a book titled Fama Fraternitatis was published anonymously in Germany, describing a global fraternity of natural philosophers, sages, and scientists devoted to studying nature. The book encouraged a spirit of camaraderie, goodwill, and unification of knowledge among its readers. Subsequently, Rosenkreuz was alleged to have assembled a small circle of enlightened men to work towards this purpose. This story is perhaps most famously outlined in the Fama Fraternitatis (1614) and later, more explicitly, in the Confessio Fraternitatis (1615).

In 1616, another book titled the Confessio was published to support Fama Fraternitatis. It was authored under the pseudonym of a mythical German adept called "C.R." or in Latin, "Christian Rosie Crucian." In these writings, Christian Rosenkreuz was presented as having come from an ancient line of German kings imbued with mystical powers. He allegedly wrote three letters and had them posted in various places around Germany. These letters described miraculous cures and helped spread his renown. They also invited others to join him in his mission.

In 1604, the third book titled The Chemical Wedding of Christian Rosenkreuz was published. This work describes a mystical and alchemical wedding. It is significant in that it includes a statement of principles that are significant as later adherents to the movement would use them. This marked the first appearance of key Rosicrucian concepts, including pansophism and Christian mysticism.

The Rosicrucians described themselves as "an order for the study of God's miracles within nature." They believed that they possessed secret wisdom and knowledge, known only to a select few. They were said to be in possession of all knowledge as set out in a secret book or "Liber Mundi" (the Book of the World). They claimed that they could travel to the inner Earth and dwell amongst the manufacturing gnomes in their self-governed utopian communities.

The Rosicrucians were known to have studied the following topics:

- Alchemy

- Astral projection

- Astrology

- Cabala (the study of esoteric Jewish mysticism)

- Hermeticism (the study of wisdom supposedly revealed by the Egyptian God Thoth, who was said to have authored The Emerald Tablet, which outlines the basis of all existence)

- Number mysticism

- Palmistry (the study of the lines on people's hands, which are believed to reveal information about that person)

- Phrenology (the study of the bumps on people's heads, which are believed to reveal information about that person)

- Reiki (an Eastern healing method)

The Significance of the Term "Rosicrucianism"

The term "Rosicrucian" or "Rose Cross" was derived from the image of rose petals encircling a cross that allegedly appeared on the cover of the Fama Fraternitatis. All of these symbols were meant to signify spiritual enlightenment. In the

Hermetic Qabalah, the "Rose Cross" is a symbol of the starry universe. It is also known as the Rose of Sharon, which grows in Palestine. The Rosicrucian Order AMORC uses this symbol in its seal.

Towards the end of the 16th century, strange literature began appearing in Europe, published by several anonymous writers under such titles as Fama Fraternitatis and Confessio Fraternitatis. These works claimed that an ancient and secret brotherhood existed behind the existing fraternities and orders, originating with the legendary Christian Rosenkreutz (1459-1523), who traveled to Damascus and was initiated into Arab occultism; returning to Europe, he established a secret order in Germany.

This alleged brotherhood was said to have maintained lodges in all parts of Europe, with a central College at Kassel in Germany. Its members were said to be bound together not only by bonds of Christian friendship and charity but also by initiation into certain mysteries handed down from generation to generation since the time of Moses.

The works also claimed the secret society had been founded and based on knowledge of alchemy, necromancy, magic, and other forbidden arts. They further declared the brotherhood had been started to oppose superstition and fanaticism, freeing mortals from the bonds of civil and religious despotism and preparing the way for the second advent of Christ upon the Earth.

Although these writings were treated as fiction, their novelty aroused widespread interest, especially as the alleged authors of the works professed a desire to establish a universal religion, harmless or helpful to all persons. At that time, Rosicrucianism's origins and purposes were unknown. It was believed to be a Secret Order of Adepts, possessing the secrets of alchemy and many other mystical arts. Its influence during this time was due to the desire of certain persons to reform society by removing the reputed evils of religious and political life.

Cultural Movement

The rose and cross emblem was believed to have been used by organizations like the Knights Templars, Rosicrucians, and Masons. Those who claimed to be members of these mysterious Orders were thought to be endowed with superhuman abilities. The movement was particularly appealing to those educated beyond the traditional Christian curriculum.

The brotherhood remained concealed for hundreds of years after it was founded. However, it is believed to have been responsible for establishing many institutions of learning which appeared in Europe throughout the the centuries preceding the Christian era. According to their writings, members had founded colleges at Oxford, Paris, Prague, Cracow, and other places.

The writings described the earlier activities of the brotherhood from its origin in ancient Egypt. According to the Fama Fraternitatis, the founders were four people who had braved death many times in their search for the great secrets of nature. They had learned universal and medicinal secrets from an Arabian sage, who himself had discovered it from still earlier philosophers among the Chaldeans, Hebrews, Persians, and Egyptians. This knowledge had been handed down through the ages to certain wise men of every nation who were made masters and deliverers of the whole world when they chose to make its power known.

In their wanderings, these sages had brought the knowledge of nature's secrets to many people; they had built cities, tilled the earth, instructed mankind in politics and ethics, discovered arts and sciences, and raised man above the beasts.

To these men, all peoples were indebted for their religions, laws, arts, sciences, even the alphabet, and the process of writing. Regardless of their country and time, all true philosophers had been members of this brotherhood, but because they had kept their knowledge secret, their fraternity had been unknown.

The story of the Rosicrucian society's origin was soon circulated throughout Germany. It was widely believed that such a society did exist and its members were pledged to lead blameless lives, practice the virtues of brotherly love, and devote themselves to the study of science, philosophy, and religion. The Rosicrucian myth was so captivating that it spread rapidly.

The early movement attracted such men as Johann Valentin Andrea (1586-1654), a Lutheran clergyman, and Michael Maier (1568-1622), a physician of Würzburg. The former was the author of several treatises on Rosicrucianism, which he defended at the universities of Jena and Leipzig. Maier, who had written on alchemy, was strongly influenced by the Rosicrucians and wrote other works on the subject.

Johann Rahn (1622-1676), a schoolteacher, published a book on the secret society entitled Teutschen Reichs-Admiral. In this work, he wrote that the biblical patriarch Enoch established the society and that its members possessed great wealth and superhuman powers. The book had enjoyed a wide circulation, and Germany believed that the brotherhood had extensive political influence extending to all parts of Europe.

Spiritual Movement

Not all attracted to the new movement were interested in learning about the secret society. Some sought spiritual guidance, and others only wanted mystic experiences. This craving for spiritual insight was satisfied by the publication of an anonymous tract entitled Christianopolis (1619), which promised to reveal the way to spiritual regeneration.

The Christianopolis was an allegory describing a journey to the City of Divine Wisdom, where, under the guidance of Wisdom, all men could learn the secret of divine light and life. The book was believed to have been written by Johann Valentin Andrea, who had combined Christian mysticism with Rosicrucian philosophy. Those who desired the mystic experience were satisfied through The Chemical Wedding (1616) and other mystical writings purported to have been written by Christian Rosenkreuz. Those who sought the former were mostly sincere seekers of divine wisdom; those who desired only the latter were looked upon as trouble-makers who used this writing to fool the public.

The movement assumed religious overtones when a pamphlet supposedly authored by the Society of Christian Rosenkreuz came to the attention of the Rosicrucians. In this document, now known as the Fama Fraternitatis, the author describes himself as a nobleman of Syria who, in about 1378, joined a band of Christian travelers who made an eastern pilgrimage to the Holy Land. While traveling through Egypt, these pilgrims were received by an old sage and given instruction on the secrets of nature. At the end of his instruction, he revealed to them a group of writings that constituted the society's secret doctrines.

This society had existed through all the ages, but it had remained unknown to outsiders because of its deep wisdom and secrecy. It was determined to make this wisdom available to all and consequently established a plan by which each society member should travel for seven years to foreign lands where he was tasked with learning to understand the mysteries of nature. At the end of this period, each member was instructed that they should go forth and spread this knowledge throughout the world.

The birth of Rosicrucianism was associated with advancing science and religious mysticism. An anonymous pamphlet entitled Fama Fraternitatis appeared in England, giving the Rosicrucians a place in history. The movement also attracted a great deal of attention in Germany, where it was believed that the Rosicrucians had a great influence on public affairs. The brotherhood was believed to have existed through all the ages and to have possessed great wealth and superhuman power.

Chapter 2: What Does It Mean to Be a Rosicrucian?

The purpose of Rosicrucianism is to encourage self-knowledge through meditation, study, and spiritual healing. The ultimate goal is human perfection through inner work and divine grace. To achieve this goal, members practice a certain system of morality and ethics. Rosicrucians are expected to be loyal, virtuous, hardworking, and independent. They have to follow certain rules and principles to be this elevated persona. This chapter will describe these vows and obligations in greater detail.

Rosicrucian Vows and Obligations

Rosicrucians follow a system of three vows and five obligations. Vows indicate what you are giving up, while obligations describe what you are committing to. The followers of Rosicrucians must take three vows to be considered a member of this movement. Vows:

1. Poverty

Rosicrucians believe that humans must not become slaves of material objects. Those who decide to become a follower of Rosicrucians must renounce all personal wealth and live with the bare minimum. This does not mean that you have to be poor. It just means that you will not possess more than the requirements and necessities in life. You must practice self-control to avoid getting caught up in the accumulation of wealth. You have to commit to living a simple life and not be distracted from the spiritual work you have to do by material possessions. You must also not keep valuables or money that will not be used for a specific purpose.

2. Chastity

All Rosicrucians are expected to be chaste and virtuous. They should be above and beyond reproach in this area. They must conduct themselves as respectable members of society, avoiding the temptations of the opposite sex. The followers of Rosicrucians are expected to be faithful to their spouses and avoid sexual contact with any other people. If a member of the Rosicrucians follows this rule, they will become a better person. If not, it is likely they will develop perversions.

3. Obedience

The followers of Rosicrucianism are expected to obey the rules and regulations of their Order to the letter. Though they have a high level of independence, they also have a certain degree of obligation. The vows indicate that the follower will renounce personal wealth and live a simple life. They also commit to living a virtuous and chaste lifestyle. This means that it might be harder for the member to do certain things because other people will not approve of them. But a true follower of Rosicrucianism is expected to do things that other people might not approve of because if they do not follow the vows, they might turn to vices and fall from grace.

Obligations

The rules include a commitment to personal honesty and a rejection of greed, envy, lust, and vanity. Obligations are promises to fulfill certain duties. These demands are laid out in the rules of each Order. There are five obligations that every follower of Rosicrucianism must abide by to move up the ranks and reach their full potential. These rules define the foundation of Rosicrucian principles. They are designed to help the member in their spiritual growth and progress.

1. Do No Evil

The followers of Rosicrucianism must be honest and trustworthy. By practicing this virtue, they will develop a sense of self-discipline. This obligation requires the member to avoid any activity which is considered sinful or hurtful to others. They should also avoid words or actions that can be considered disgraceful and offensive to others. If a member of Rosicrucians acts in such a way, they will be held accountable for their deeds, and they will also be held accountable for their actions if they try to justify them by saying, "everyone else is doing it."

2. Do Good

Rosicrucian members are expected to act with kindness and respect towards others. Their superiors will them responsible if they do not abide by this obligation. The followers of Rosicrucianism must positively influence society and help others to the best of their ability. They should promote and support good health, education, and social reform. It is also important that they promote peace and equality among all members of society. This obligation might affect how the member acts in the public eye because they must follow this code to maintain their vows and reach spiritual enlightenment.

3. Serve the Order

Rosicrucian members must put the needs of their Order before their own. They should be willing to help others, and they should also be eager to contribute to their community and society. This obligation requires the member to put aside personal desires to serve others and not be selfish with resources or time. The members should also be willing to promote the ideals and principles of their Order. The Rosicrucians understand that putting others before themselves makes them better people, which will make it easier to follow the next two obligations.

4. Deny Oneself

The members of Rosicrucianism are expected to take care of their bodies. They should practice moderation and self-control when eating, drinking, and even engaging in sexual activity. They should also avoid any behavior that may be harmful to their mental and physical well-being. This part of the obligation might be the hardest as members will be expected to practice total abstinence if they wish to move up in their Order.

5. Seek the Truth

The members of Rosicrucianism must be open to learning, and they should always thirst for knowledge and must be willing to learn new things, which will equip them to practice the other four obligations. The Rosicrucians explain that this obligation is necessary to understand other people, which will help them avoid certain sins and behaviors.

Fulfilling the five obligations will allow the member to move closer to reaching spiritual enlightenment. They should also know that there is no "self-help" path or shortcut to spiritual enlightenment as it is a lifelong practice. They have to follow these tenets to close any open doors that may lead them down the path to temptation and evil.

Rosicrucianism is a belief system that combines Gnosticism and Hermeticism into one. In other words, it is a combination of knowledge and faith. The main goal of this group is for its members to gain knowledge about creation through an experience called illumination. This can be achieved through different ways such as meditation, chanting, or even music and dance. There are two paths members can choose to follow to achieve illumination: Gnosticism or Hermeticism.

Gnosticism

The followers of the Gnostic movement are expected to believe in a strict moral code. The Gnostics believe that a demon created the physical world in opposition to God. They also believe that all humans are born evil because of their connection with the physical world. To become closer with God and reach spiritual enlightenment, the members must make sacrifices to separate themselves from their evil nature. The members of Rosicrucianism need to practice celibacy and abstinence. They should also avoid any type of materialism because they must not be attached to anything in this world.

When members do gain spiritual illumination, they are expected to act as an example of the entire Rosicrucian movement. They should be moral and serve as a guide to others. To remain a member, they must practice what they preach and live by the Rosicrucian code of conduct. The members must also vow to keep the spiritual knowledge they have gained secret because it is not meant for everyone. If they do not follow these guidelines, they risk losing their blessings and enlightenment.

Hermeticism

The Hermetic members believe that God is a being of pure love, and the physical world is the only way to reach him. They believe that everyone has a divine spark inside of them, and it can be awakened through different methods. Hermetic followers reject the idea that people are born evil and believe humans can make choices. They also believe in finding true happiness through love. The members have different rituals to help them get closer to God. For example, the followers of Hermeticism may go on a retreat in the woods where they meditate and chant.

The followers of the Hermetic movement are expected to believe in a "religion of the stars," meaning they should look to the stars for their guidance. One of the reasons for this is because they believe that God is in everything, including the planets and stars. By studying the movements of the stars, they can gain knowledge and wisdom. They also believe that there is a hierarchy among different groups to understand the divine better. For example, seven angels are higher in rank than humans.

Members of the Hermetic movement are expected to live a life in harmony with nature. They should also live in unity with the community and help others. One example of this is that they must give a gift to a fellow member regularly. The gift can be money, knowledge, or even time. They also have a strict moral code. For example, a Hermetic follower should not lie and must always do their best to become one with the universe.

Gnosticism vs. Hermeticism

The main difference between the Gnostic and Hermetic ways of life is that the followers of the Gnostic movement believe in strict moral codes. In contrast, the members of Hermetics believe in living a life of nature and unity within the community. However, they do both agree that the ultimate goal is to experience illumination. There are also different paths that members can choose to achieve this enlightenment. Once they have reached the state of illumination, they believe that a certain deity is activated. The members of the Gnostic movement will have a different deity than those of Hermetics.

The path chosen by an individual will determine if they are allowed to pursue another obligation. For example, the members of Rosicrucianism who follow the sub-sect, Hermeticism, are allowed to get married and have a family. On the other hand, those who follow the path of Gnosticism are allowed to get married, but they must practice celibacy. A member who chooses not to follow either path does not have to get married. They can pursue another obligation such as being a vegetarian, avoiding drugs and alcohol, or even becoming a vegan.

In conclusion, the Rosicrucians have five obligations that all followers must abide by to live a moral and virtuous life. It is important to understand the meaning behind these obligations because they guide the members to a path of enlightenment and spiritual awareness. By becoming a member, individuals can gain knowledge and understanding about the world around them. It is also important to understand that these obligations are not mandatory, as long as they choose a path of life that will guide them to spiritual enlightenment.

Chapter 3: Rosicrucian Organizations and Manifestos

In the early 17th century, a group of mystics and scholars gathered in Germany to spread the teachings of a belief system they called Rosicrucianism. These people called for a reformation of science, religion, and government; however, their true identity was never revealed. Toward the end of the 18th century, rumors had spread about the existence of a secret society that held knowledge about life, nature, and the universe. This made people believe that such knowledge was attainable. Several organizations were formed to share this knowledge in response to this curiosity. This chapter discusses the origins of Rosicrucian organizations and briefly discusses their beliefs.

Three Early Rosicrucian Societies

One of the earliest known associations based on the Rose Cross was formed in 1614 by J.V. Andreae, a Lutheran theologian. This association was named Confraternitatem R.C., the Confraternity of the Rose Cross, and was formed in Strasbourg. Andreae became interested in seeing a reformation within society and used the symbol of the rose cross to represent his ideas about it.

Another early group that called itself Rosicrucian was the Brothers of Christian Reunion. This society was formed in France by Stephen Dadault, who claimed to be an initiate of a German Rosicrucian fraternity located near Württemberg. Little is known about the group other than that it had several members who were persecuted during 1711.

The third early Rosicrucian society was the Hermetic Order of the Golden Dawn, which was formed in London in 1888 by William Wynn Westcott. The Order claimed to have been founded on the remains of a secret Rosicrucian order in Germany. It had three degrees that were based on alchemy and kabbalah. Within the Order, members tried to contact spiritual beings and understand the mysteries of life and nature.

Primary Beliefs of Rosicrucian Organizations

The primary beliefs of Rosicrucian organizations focus on achieving perfection to attain higher knowledge that will ultimately lead to happiness and eternal salvation. These groups believed that one should take the initiative to practice virtue, wisdom, and benevolence, which lead to becoming an adept or master who has attained knowledge of nature, the universe, and God.

The society's members were referred to as "initiates" because they believed that only those who had undergone initiation could grasp their ideas about nature, the universe, and life. They believed that different degrees of initiations occurred during one's physical and spiritual life and that after death, the initiate would experience the "second birth." This initiation process allowed them to receive divine knowledge and helped them acquire supernatural abilities such as communicating with spirits.

The adepts or masters were those members of a society who had achieved perfection. These members were promoted within the Order's hierarchy and served as teachers to those beginners initiated into the society. The idea was that if one took the time to become like an adept or master, they would attain knowledge about nature, life, and God, bringing them closer to having all knowledge of mankind's past, present, and future.

The concept of reincarnation was another core belief of Rosicrucian organizations. They believed that one's soul is reborn after death, and each time the person died, they would be reborn with a new body and given a new chance to put their knowledge into practice. Each incarnation gave them more opportunities to advance spiritually, bringing them closer to perfection. Karma is another belief associated with reincarnation. They believed that karma resulted from actions performed during one's life and that these would be carried into the next reincarnation.

Rosicrucian organizations also recognized the idea of a great white brotherhood that served as guardians and protectors of the world. It is believed that this group was eventually formed as a result of the Rosicrucian society.

The Tree of Life was another primary belief associated with Rosicrucian organizations. It is an important symbol for Kabbalah and represents the process needed to achieve divine knowledge and eternal happiness. The ten spheres or sephiroth on this tree represent the ten manifestations of divinity and enlightenment. By studying this symbolism, they believed that one could learn about God and life's mysteries.

It is also believed that Rosicrucian societies hold most of the ancient wisdom of alchemy, astrology, and magic. These claims are based on the belief that many members of these organizations were the inventors of modern-day science.

The primary objectives for Rosicrucian societies were to grow in knowledge towards perfection in three spheres, nature, life, and God, and to perfect their spiritual, mental, and physical selves. They were expected to contribute positively to society through benevolence and charity, enlighten others by sharing wisdom learned throughout their experiences, and ultimately achieve their self-perfection through service to others.

Rosicrucian Manifestos

Fama Fraternitatis Rosae Crucis

The first one is the Fama Fraternitatis Rosae Crucis, published in 1614 in Kassel, Germany. It contained an alleged letter from a Frater C.R.C., who supposedly lived in Germany during the early 15th century. He tells about a secret society that met in the "Egyptian desert" and was founded on 29 May 1378. This society built (or re-built) some kind of Temple or Abbey, called "Collegium ad Spiritum Sanctum," which would be later known as "The House of the Holy Spirit." The author of the manifest says that he was present at this building ceremony in 1402 and that this brother was called Christian

Rosenkreutz. This name is also used as a pseudonym for one of the authors. However, it is hard to say if there was such a person or if he is just an allegory or a composite of different persons.

When the manifest came out, it caused quite a stir because it claimed that Christian Rosenkreutz had traveled through many countries spreading knowledge about the natural sciences and alchemy, especially knowledge about prolonging human life. He supposedly started his travels in 1394, went to Italy to study the secrets of the art of memory and natural magic, then continued his travels through Greece and Spain. During his stay in Spain, he learned about the secret knowledge of alchemy and met a Muslim man who taught him the art of transmutation. After this, he returned to Germany and founded the Rosicrucian Society. He then went on another journey to Damascus (Syria), where he worked as a spy.

After many travels, he returned to Germany and died at a ripe old age of 106. It is believed he was buried in a secret tomb, with an alchemist symbol sealing the entrance. A year later, the inscription "Hic Grates Natus" (here grateful to the birth of) was added, and another year later, another inscription "Anno 1459" (the year 1459).

After many years had passed, the entrance was opened again, and the mystic rose engraved on his tombstone seemed to be fresh and fragrant, as if it had just been freshly cut.

The manifest claims that the society of Rosicrucians continued to exist and propagate knowledge over time, but they would only show themselves to those who practiced alchemy and magic. It is said that they give advice and help on many things such as healing, talismans and share their knowledge about nature.

Confessio Fraternitatis

The second manifesto was called Confessio Fraternitatis Rosae Crucis, published in 1615. It contained much of the same information as Fama but added more details about their society and its history. This one specifically says that Christian Rosenkreutz was born in 1378 in a city called "Rosenberg" (which means "Rose Mountain" in German) and that he was a person of great learning. According to this manifesto, Christian Rosenkreutz was a member of the "first true and original order of Rosicrucians," which he later reformed around 1378.

The manifesto claims that so many people joined Rosenkreutz in his Order, that their number increased significantly. During this time, the

Turkish Empire was expanding and spreading out into different regions of Europe, which caused great concern to Christian Rosenkreutz and his followers. They were afraid that the Turks would spread Islam throughout Europe, which they thought would be a disaster for Christianity.

They decided to infiltrate Turkey to learn the secrets of the Muslim culture, and when they returned, they started preaching what they had learned from their enemies to people in Germany. They also wrote a book called Turris Babel (Tower of Babel), a warning against religious conflicts in Europe, claiming that this would be one of the causes that could lead to a disaster for humanity.

The manifesto claims that the number of members in their society grew to well over 2,000 people. Some of them were rich merchants and various princes. Many rulers sent delegations to Christian Rosenkreutz to learn the secret knowledge held by his group, so much so that he had to build a large house for everyone. According to the manifesto, many people tried to join his Order but found it difficult because of the strict rules they had to keep. This house became known as 'The House of the Holy Spirit,' and its members were called 'The Invisibles.'

In 1604, Christian Rosenkreutz died at a very old age knowing that his mission had been accomplished. After his death, members continued to spread wisdom and knowledge until the manifest was published in 1614.

The Chymical Wedding of Christian Rosenkreutz

The last Rosicrucian manifesto was called Chymical Wedding of Christian Rosenkreutz. It was published in 1616, which means it came out after Confessio Fraternitatis and Fama's second edition. The author is unknown but assumed to be Johann Valentin Andreae, author of major works written during the heyday of the Rosicrucian movement.

Like previous manifestos, this one describes the life of Christian Rosenkreutz and his adventures in the East, where he studied with wise men. While he was there, he learned about alchemy and the role of religion in society.

This manifesto describes Christian Rosenkreutz's initiation into a mysterious temple in Damcar, where he was separated from his body and experienced a mystical journey. In this experience, he meets the king of the world, who describes the secrets of the universe and how it came to be.

In this text, Christian Rosenkreutz is given a series of alchemical formulas he learned after his initiation. He then returned to the House of the Holy Spirit, where he started preparing for a wedding ceremony held in the spiritual world and visible on Earth. During this ceremony, he transmitted all of his knowledge to his followers, and then he died.

The Chymical Wedding of Christian Rosenkreutz was written to explain the true meaning of alchemy and its role in society. It describes how alchemists can use their knowledge to transform themselves into perfect human beings and explains the role of religion in this process.

After exploring these three manifestos, one can see the origins of Rosicrucianism and how its members spread their knowledge to different parts of Europe. The first manifesto shows how they spread knowledge about the symbolic meaning of alchemy, the second one talks about accessing secret knowledge and their aims, and the last one describes how this information was transmitted.

As a whole, these manifestos were a way for Rosicrucian groups to come together and spread a common message. They wanted to promote the knowledge this movement held and attract new members who would help them achieve their goals and spread their ideas all over Europe.

Chapter 4: The Rosicrucian Sign

The Rosicrucian Sign is an ancient symbol used since the ages of antiquity. In modern times, it is also known as the Rose Cross. It's a symbol that several different religions have adopted, and many use it in their churches and places of worship. Taken as a whole, the Rose Cross is a powerful and meaningful symbol that represents the balance between active and passive energies. This makes it a valuable symbol for people to incorporate in some way into their lives. This chapter will explore the individual elements in the sign and how they collectively merge to become this powerful sign.

The Sign of the Rose Cross

The Rose Cross or Rosy Cross is a symbol of the Rosicrucian Order. It consists of a golden cross with a red rose at its center. The cross represents the infinite nature of God, and the rose is symbolic of the human soul. The Rose Cross symbolizes man's journey from earthly life to spiritual enlightenment, from death to eternal life. It also represents the balance between active and passive energies.

The cross and the rose have both been used for centuries as symbols for different things. The cross is known for its power as a religious symbol. The shape of the Celtic cross, for example, has been found in artifacts dating back to 300 BCE. The rose was an important symbol in ancient alchemical texts because it represented regeneration through the cycle of nature and seasons.

The two symbols represent opposite ends of the human experience: the cross represents mortality, while the rose represents immortality. In fact, during medieval times, Christian monks often used a similar symbol — they combined a skull with a rosary, which represented how faith can help us endure moments of death with hope for eternal life.

In 18th century Europe, many people were starting to question traditional beliefs and institutions that had dominated Europe for centuries, including Christianity and its promise of eternal life for all who accepted its doctrines. The changes sweeping through society at this time naturally had a big impact on religion and led to the formation of many alternatives to Christian denominations, one such being the Rosicrucians.

The Rosy Cross is the symbol of this Fraternity. It is composed of a cross above a rose and is at the same time a cross of roses. The man who discovered it was Count Robert von Hütten, a Rosicrucian Initiate who lived in the first quarter of the eighteenth century. He combined, in his way, the Rose, representing passive wisdom, with the Cross that represented active wisdom (the heart and brain). This sign was adopted by all subsequent members and incorporated into their seals. It became known as the emblem of the Order and remains so to this day.

The Rose

In Rosicrucianism, the rose represents the human soul because it is a delicate, beautiful thing that contains nectar representing divine knowledge. The petals of the rose are thought to represent the five senses possessed by humans. The rose was revered as a symbol of regeneration, making it an appropriate symbol for Rosicrucianism, a movement based on spiritual rebirth.

The rose was also symbolic in the art of alchemy; it symbolized the achievement of perfection and immortality through the purification of base metals into gold. As an important symbol in alchemy, it was given significance through representing the Philosopher's Stone. It is also the symbol of love and secrecy — two central themes of alchemy.

Between the 12th and 14th centuries, the rose became synonymous with the Virgin Mary in Christianity. The red color of roses symbolized the life and blood of Jesus, while the white color symbolized his purity. The rose became a symbol of female virginity, an important role that Mary played in Christianity. The rose was also used as the symbol of the Order, which added to its importance and symbolism because, as a fraternal group, women were not allowed to join.

The rose has always been seen as a positive and lucky symbol, and is one of the most powerful symbols you can use. Those who have a particular fondness for roses will find that incorporating this powerful symbol into their lives can help bring them good fortune and health.

The Cross

The cross has been a religious symbol for thousands of years and, in its design, represents the four directions of north, south, east, and west. These four points symbolize the spiritual realm intersecting with our physical world, and it has been featured prominently in many places around the world, including churches, graveyards, and public spaces. It has been used as a religious symbol by almost every major religion, including Christianity, Buddhism, Hinduism, Islam, and ancient Egyptian religions.

The cross is thought to represent the four cardinal virtues of justice, prudence, temperance, and fortitude. It also represents the four gospels of Matthew, Mark, Luke, and John, which are held to be the cornerstone of Christian belief. The cross is also thought to represent the five wounds that Jesus suffered during his crucifixion, including his crown of thorns and pierced hands and feet. This reference to Jesus' suffering ties in closely with the rose because it represents a divine knowledge of God that can lead humanity to eternal life through contemplation (like meditation).

The cross has many different meanings but, in Rosicrucianism, it represents the beginning of wisdom and spiritual rebirth. The cross is the Qabalistic sign of Tiphereth, which lies at the center of the Tree of Life. It is also the alchemical symbol for Sulphur, one of the three primes that make up the alchemical process. In Freemasonry, the Tau cross is a symbol of life and immortality, similar to its representation in Rosicrucianism. When a circle surrounds it, it represents the Sun being encircled by the four elements of earth, wind, fire, and water. The cross has become a powerful symbol over the years, and it is sure to continue as more religions are created.

The Rosy Cross

The rose and the cross combined to create a powerful symbol recognized by many different religions and people. This symbol, known as the Rosy Cross, was first documented in 1614 as a symbol of secrecy. In the text, titled Fama Fraternitatis, it was written that the symbol could be found on a banner of those who lived in Rosicrucian-influenced German states. Although the Rosicrucians were a secret society that did not reveal their identities, other symbols found in Europe have been associated with them.

The first known symbol of the Rosy Cross was a large cross surrounded by a circle and an encircled dot or 'i'. The cross represented Christianity as it is also known as the Christian symbol, and the circle represented eternity because of its continuous nature. The encircled 'i' or dot is thought to indicate that we are all one and part of God's creation.

Later, the Christian symbol was altered slightly and became more like a cross with a single rose in the center. It is said to be made up of three crosses, representing the Father, Son, and Holy Ghost. These three crosses are then surrounded by a circle of roses depicting the five wounds that Jesus experienced during his crucifixion. Five roses are also said to represent the five senses of sight, smell, touch, taste, and hearing, while twelve petals were thought to represent the Apostles and seven leaves represented the Seven Liberal Arts and Seven Sacraments.

The new symbol also had some similarities in alchemy as it was inscribed into a pentagram. A pentagram is a five-sided star representing the relationships between earth and the other elements - water, air, fire, and quintessence. The Rosy Cross has been used in many applications, including flags, banners, and personal adornment. The Rosicrucian Fellowship is also known to use as their official seal.

The fact that so many different religions have used the symbol of the cross proves just how powerful its symbolism truly is. The five interconnected crosses represent Jesus' suffering and death while also representing God's love for humanity. The circle surrounding the cross shows that God's love is eternal and surrounds us at all times. The rose in the center of the cross brings together Christian symbolism with alchemy as its five petals represent Jesus' wounds while also representing the five elements- earth, air, fire, water, and quintessence (which is the highest element).

The Rosicrucians later decided to replace the five interconnected crosses with a single cross and a single rose, representing Christ's one body and soul and his second coming. This symbol was also inscribed in a pentagram, and it became even more popular than its predecessor. Today, the most common symbol is the one inscribed in a pentagram, and its connection to alchemy has been widely regarded.

The truly fascinating part of this symbol is that it has been connected to multiple different religions, which shows how powerful its symbolism is. The symbolism is also found in Freemasonry. Depending on where it's being used, it has many different names, but it is most commonly referred to as the Rosicrucian cross.

The symbols, associations, and religious connections found within the Rosicrucian sign are what makes it so significant. Its original association with secret societies and religious figures has given it a mysterious quality, but its symbolism is so universal that everyone can recognize it as a sign of love, life, Christianity, and all things holy.

Chapter 5: Rosicrucianism Today

We live in a time where spirituality is expressed in many different ways. With so many religions, beliefs, philosophies, and concepts to choose from, it can be rather difficult to find one that fits you exactly.

The Rosicrucian Order AMORC was established in 1915 by its founder H. Spencer Lewis in San Jose, California. It was the first Rosicrucian Order ever created and still holds great significance for its members today. Rosicrucianism is often perceived as an ancient belief system with origins dating back to the middle ages. It has roots in many philosophical and religious ideas, which is why it is rather difficult to define Rosicrucianism without delving into the history of it all. This chapter highlights how Rosicrucianism is perceived today, how it is molded and how these can be traced back to the past.

The Evolution of Rosicrucianism

The most prominent of all the Western Esoteric and Occult philosophies, Rosicrucianism is a modern Hermetic tradition. It is based on the existence of an actual Rosicrucian Brotherhood that enigmatically appeared at the beginning of the seventeenth century and was, for a short time, quite visible and influential in European politics. Toward the end of the seventeenth century, the Rosicrucian influence was still powerful and visible in Masonic lodges.

Rosicrucianism has evolved; it is not a static doctrine or belief system. The evolution of this philosophy can be traced by looking at its influences throughout time. Although there is no single source for Rosicrucian beliefs, several groups have contributed to its development through history. As an organized movement or society, Rosicrucianism first appeared with the document Fama Fraternitatis in 1614, but its disorganized origins dated from the Middle Ages when alchemists sought more than just material knowledge. It combines many different beliefs into one, coming from many different religious influences. It is important to know that Rosicrucians are not limited to regularly following just one religion but can take bits of information from each branch of belief. Rosicrucianism is a philosophy for all types of people from all walks of life.

How Rosicrucianism Is Perceived Today

Rosicrucianism is perceived today as a modern Hermetic tradition, which means that it has the same views as Hermeticism, with an added focus on alchemy. This includes multiple different elements from various religions, philosophies, and cultures. The direct methods of influence and control of the organization in the past are not used today, but there is still a definite structure in place. The more you learn about Rosicrucianism, the more you will understand that there are many levels to one's involvement in this group. The teachings of this group are passed down from teacher to student, and that there is no official creed or study guide available for anyone to purchase.

Many people exposed to the Rosicrucian teachings will say that certain books do a good job of explaining the basics, but these books were written by people who have studied Rosicrucianism for many years. This does not have to be a bad thing because Rosicrucian philosophy is flexible enough so that anyone who studies it will come up with different conclusions based on their personal experiences. Therefore, this tradition is not difficult to understand, but you should try to find a teacher if you are interested in gaining access to the information.

How Rosicrucianism Is Molded Today

One of the biggest issues currently facing Rosicrucianism today is the fact that it is not just an organization but also a philosophy. This means that many different ideas and theories guide how a modern Rosicrucian thinks and behaves. These belief systems have been adopted through the years to become part of a long and ongoing tradition. This has resulted in the creation of many different branches of Rosicrucian beliefs not always consistent with one another. This does cause some problems at times, but it has created a way for Rosicrucians to have many different views on the same subject. This helps them to understand things in a more diverse manner, which is a strength.

The manifestos do not concentrate on this world but on another, a mystical, spiritual, and divine reality that a transformed and purified mind can reach. They claimed that by applying the highest of human faculties achievable through the development of the physical body and human consciousness, one might achieve " illumination, "enabling the direct experience of the divine, cosmic truths and so become more godlike.

Their texts claim that this knowledge had originally been known to humanity and passed down for thousands of years by a succession of great prophets: Zoroaster, Moses, Hermes Trismegistus, Christianity's Jesus Christ, Muhammad, and others.

The modern Rosicrucian philosophy has become more of an amalgamation of different religious belief systems that have been combined into a larger coherent whole. This includes representatives from all of the major religions throughout history, but Rosicrucians do not follow any one of them exclusively. Instead, they are inspired by many different belief systems, picking the parts that work for them and discarding the other parts. This is why there are so many different branches of Rosicrucianism today because each person who becomes involved with the group will find something that speaks to them and incorporate that into their belief system.

How Rosicrucianism Is Traced from the Past

No one person or event can be traced back to how Rosicrucianism started, but many different people have influenced the course of this group's history. Some of the most influential people throughout history have been Pythagoras,

Leonardo da Vinci, Sir Francis Bacon, Gottfried Wilhelm Leibniz, and Christian Rosenkreuz. All of these people have been used to trace the historical development of Rosicrucianism, but not all of them were a direct influence.

Christian Rosenkreuz is the primary figure associated with Rosicrucianism, but he is also not taken that seriously by many people involved with the group. The legend says that this man lived for 106 years and was able to gain an incredible amount of wisdom during that time. He then founded the Rosicrucian Order in the late 1400s and died shortly after that. There are no records of the man at all during his supposed lifetime, which means that he is a completely fabricated figure.

Nonetheless, the idea of Christian Rosenkreuz has been important throughout Rosicrucian history, so much so that his symbol is even part of the Rosicrucian seal. This man has been one of the most important historical figures for Rosicrucianism, but it makes more sense when you understand that this man has been used to represent the myth itself. This is not a historical figure; instead, he is an integral part of the Rosicrucian myths.

What Are the Modern Rosicrucianism Beliefs?

Modern Rosicrucianism is all about the balance of good and evil. They believe that everything has an opposite, so it is important for people to understand how to handle both. This is what makes good people good and bad people bad because both exist in the same person. Life has a way of balancing itself out in the end when people do not try to tip the scales in their favor. This is why Rosicrucians believe that it is important to be good people and try to make the world a better place.

The Rosicrucian Order has been broken up into many different branches, each with its own beliefs. Some of them are more spiritual, while others believe that they can create change in the world through political means. Many of them have been able to coexist well with modern society without attracting too much attention of any kind - negative or positive. This is because they do not want to bring about any controversy and instead want to focus on doing what is right for society as a whole.

The Order of the Rose Cross is one of the largest branches of modern Rosicrucianism. This group has lodges all over the world and focuses on what is best for the individual. They believe in personal development through higher education, so they encourage people to go out and learn about the world around them. The Order of the Rose Cross also focuses on inner peace, which is why they believe that each person should work on themselves before trying to fix the world around them.

Rosicrucianism has evolved completely throughout modern history, so much so that it can no longer be linked to its past. This is part of the reason why there are so many different branches, each with its own beliefs. Even though they all come from the same source, they do not necessarily think that the other branches are right. This has been a big part of Rosicrucianism in the modern era because it no longer has the same meaning as it first started.

Modern Rosicrucians are trying to bring about change for the betterment of society. This may not be seen as important by everyone, but this group provides insight into the world that you would not be able to get otherwise. This group does not see itself as one group, but instead, many different branches focusing on different parts of the world. They all believe in helping people live their best lives, but they also know that this cannot happen if people are unwilling to do the work. This is why they focus so heavily on education and what it means to become a truly enlightened person.

Rosicrucianism's evolution does not mean they can distance themselves entirely from what has happened in the past, but it is now more focused on the future than anything else. This means they cannot continue to use Christian Rosenkreuz to initiate people because he is now just an important figure or figment of imagination from the past. This has been a big part of Rosicrucianism because they know that they cannot continue to teach and represent the same thing throughout history.

Today, Rosicrucianism is not as popular as it once was. It has transformed into a different kind of group that focuses more on bringing about change in the world than on bringing people into a bigger picture. The Order of the Rose Cross knows that it cannot continue to be the same group that it once was because too many changes have taken place in the world. Even though this group does not have the same power and authority it once did, they are still working towards the same goal: to make the world a better place through education and knowledge.

Conclusion

Rosicrucianism's name comes from the Order's emblem, the Rosy Cross. It is symbolized by a red cross with a rose in the center, often depicted on a white background. The origins of this symbol come from the legend of Christian Rosenkreuz, who was said to have created it while searching for a hidden vault containing knowledge.

The Order itself was said to be founded in 1407 by Christian Rosenkreuz with the publication of Fama Fraternitatis RC (The Discovery of the Fraternity of R: C). This work announced to all that a fraternity called "The Brothers of R: C" had been founded in Germany two years prior and that it had existed for centuries before being re-established. The story further explains that its members were engaged in studying alchemy and spagyrics, among other things. The purpose of the fraternity was to investigate the secrets of nature and, in doing so, also investigate how this knowledge might be used for humankind's benefit.

This guide explains what Rosicrucianism is, what it means to be a member of this fraternity and the significance of its symbol. The first chapter talked about the origins of

Rosicrucianism and how it was believed to have been founded. During the first years of its existence, the Order was relatively unknown, but after the publication of Fama Fraternitatis RC, it became more popular.

The second chapter discussed what being a Rosicrucian means and how that relates to the Order. Those interested in joining the Order needed to be initiated, meaning an initiate had to be tested and work their way up from a lower degree to a higher degree. The initiation process depended on which order a person was interested in joining.

The third chapter introduced the reader to some of the organizations connected with Rosicrucianism. These organizations include the Confraternity of the Rose Cross, Brothers of Christian Reunion, and the Hermetic Order of the Golden Dawn. This chapter covered the different Rosicrucian Manifestos in history, their main focus, and core beliefs.

In the fourth chapter, the reader learns about the Rosy Cross symbol that members of the Order use. The rose and the cross were described as having special meaning, and even today, these signs can be found in many places. The symbol comes from a legend about Christian Rosenkreuz, who is said to have founded the fraternity. He traveled around Asia and the Middle East, where he learned a great deal about different cultures and their religions.

The fifth and final chapter focused on Rosicrucianism today. This chapter explained that the Order is continuing today, and it discusses how the current movement of Rosicrucianism compares to what it was in the past. People can join by simply purchasing a certificate or having someone vouch for them. It was also explained that there are still divisions between different Rosicrucian societies. However, despite these disagreements, the chapter did point out that all modern Rosicrucian societies share the same basic principles.

After reading this guide, it becomes clear that Rosicrucianism is an order with a long history. Its symbol is related to Christianity, and its members have a great interest in alchemy, spagyrics, and other scientific topics. The Order is still around today, and it has changed some of its beliefs and practices since its first appearance.

References

Books, L. L. C. (2011). Rosicrucianism: Alexandru Bogdan-Pite Ti, Rosy Cross, Rosicrucian Monographs, the Rosicrucian Cosmo-Conception, Fama Fraternitatis (L. L. C. Books, Ed.). Books LLC, Wiki Series.

McIntosh, C. (1992). Chapter two: Rosicrucianism from its origins to the early 18th century. In The Rose Cross and the Age of Reason (pp. 23–37). BRILL.

What is Rosicrucianism? (2006, May 21). GotQuestions.Org. https://www.gotquestions.org/Rosicrucianism.html

(N.d.-a). Psu.Edu. Retrieved from http://citeseerx.ist.psu.edu/viewdoc/download?doi=10.1.1 .693.552&rep=rep1&type=pdf

Books, L. L. C. (2011). Rosicrucianism: Alexandru Bogdan-Pite Ti, Rosy Cross, Rosicrucian Monographs, the Rosicrucian Cosmo-Conception, Fama Fraternitatis (L. L. C. Books, Ed.). Books LLC, Wiki Series.

McIntosh, C. (1992). Chapter two: Rosicrucianism from its origins to the early 18th century. In The Rose Cross and the Age of Reason (pp. 23–37). BRILL.

What is Rosicrucianism? (2006, May 21). GotQuestions.Org. https://www.gotquestions.org/Rosicrucianism.html

(N.d.-a). Psu.Edu. Retrieved from http://citeseerx.ist.psu.edu/viewdoc/download?doi=10.1.1 .693.552&rep=rep1&type=pdf

Bebergal, P. (2016, October 26). Reimagining a shadowy medieval brotherhood that probably didn't exist. New Yorker (New York, N.Y.: 1925). https://www.newyorker.com/books/page-turner/reimagining-a-shadowy-medieval-brotherhood-that-probably-didnt-exist

de Vries, L. (2021). Rosicrucianism praised: The early response. In Reformation, Revolution, Renovation (pp. 215–291). BRILL.

Ruby, C. D. (Ed.). (2011). Ancient Mystical Order Rosae Crucis. Fidel.

The Rosicrucian Order, AMORC. (n.d.). The Rosicrucian Order, AMORC. Retrieved from https://www.rosicrucian.org/

(N.d.-a). Researchgate.Net. Retrieved from https://www.researchgate.net/publication/349862080_THE_ROSICRUCIAN_MANIFESTOS_AND_EARLY_ROSICRUCIANISM

(N.d.-b). Diva-Portal.Se. Retrieved from http://www.diva-portal.se/smash/get/diva2:1427453/FULLTEXT01.pdf

Behold the sign: Ancient Symbolism by Ralph M. lewis. (n.d.). The Rosicrucian Order, AMORC. Retrieved from https://www.rosicrucian.org/rosicrucian-books-behold-the-sign-ancient-symbolism

Beyer, C. (n.d.). What does the Rosy Cross Mean? Learn Religions. Retrieved from https://www.learnreligions.com/the-rosy-cross-or-rose-cross-95997

Rosa, S. [UCxBOacBOtgcIKyTxCoeiBHA]. (2019, August 21). Secret Symbols of the Rosicrucians. Youtube. https://www.youtube.com/watch?v=yprigy6jWgk

The Rose Cross: History and symbolism. (2021, July 8). Symbol Sage. https://symbolsage.com/rose-cross-history-meaning/

(N.d.). Barnesandnoble.Com. Retrieved from https://www.barnesandnoble.com/w/rosicrucian-rules-secret-signs-codes-and-symbols-franz-hartmann/1137645048

Bamford, C. (n.d.). Buy The Secret Stream: Christian Rosenkreutz and Rosicrucianism book online at low prices in India. Amazon.In. Retrieved from https://www.amazon.in/Secret-Stream-Christian-Rosenkreutz-Rosicrucianism/dp/0880104759

Edition, N. S. (2015, April 19). Shadows in the shadows: The Rosicrucians, A Fake Secret society, had a real impact on the world. Newsweek. https://www.newsweek.com/fake-secret-society-secret-society-323248

McIntosh, C. (1992). Chapter two: Rosicrucianism from its origins to the early 18th century. In The Rose Cross and the Age of Reason (pp. 23–37). BRILL.

Silva, C. (2021, April 23). A centuries-old secret society is hanging out in Facebook groups. Mashable. https://mashable.com/article/rosicrucian-order-on-facebook

The Rosicrucian Order, AMORC. (n.d.). The Rosicrucian Order, AMORC. Retrieved from https://www.rosicrucian.org/

Vallely, P. (2009, August 5). Cross purposes: Who are the Rosicrucians? Independent. https://www.independent.co.uk/news/world/americas/cross-purposes-who-are-the-rosicrucians-1767848.html

What is Rosicrucianism? (2006, May 21). GotQuestions.Org. https://www.gotquestions.org/Rosicrucianism.html